I Am America

Charles R. Smith Jr.

SCHOLASTIC INC.

NEW YORK • TORONTO • LONDON • AUCKLAND • SYDNEY

MEXICO CITY • NEW DELHI • HONG KONG • BUENOS AIRES

I am
America.

I am
proud.

I am
diverse,

soft-spoken,
and loud.

I am
almond
eyes.

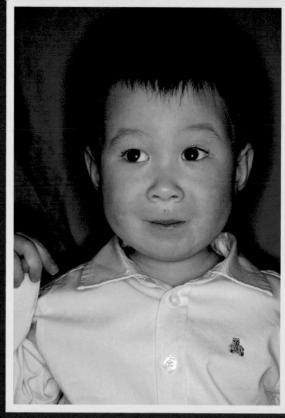

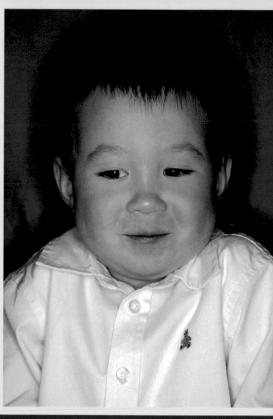

I am a
proud
nose.

I am cheeks freckled the color of a rose.

 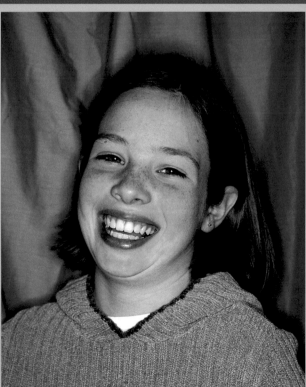 

I am
jet-
black
hair.

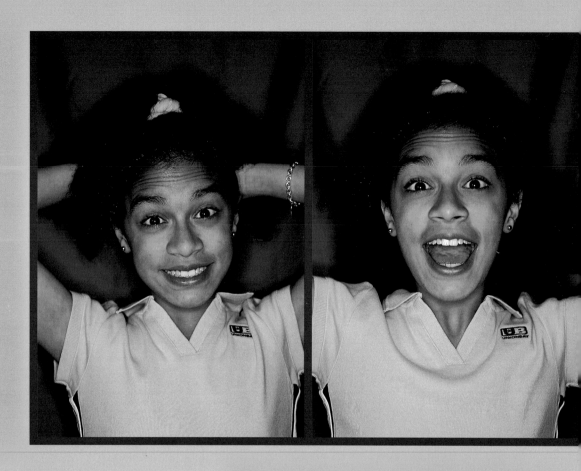

I am
olive
skin.

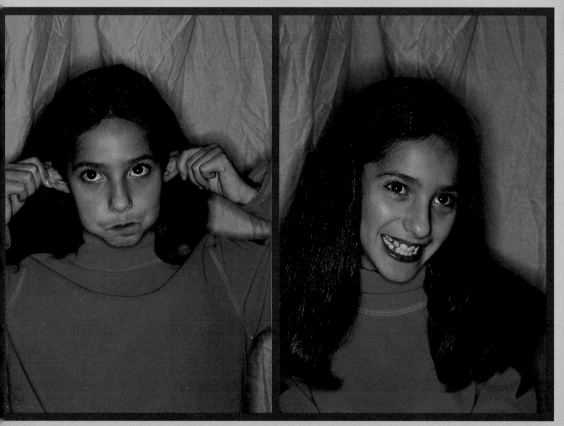

I am **my** grandfather's dimples framing my grin.

I am big baggy jeans.

I am
bandana
wraps.

I am blue denim jackets.

I am
backwards
baseball caps.

I am rhythm.

I am
blues.

I am
country.

I am
soul.

I am jazz.

I am hip-hop.

I am
grunge
rock and roll.

I am candy cane sticks.

I am
ice-cream
smiles.

I am lollipop licks.

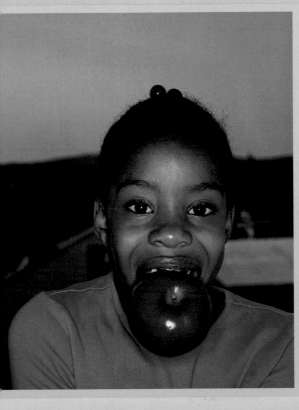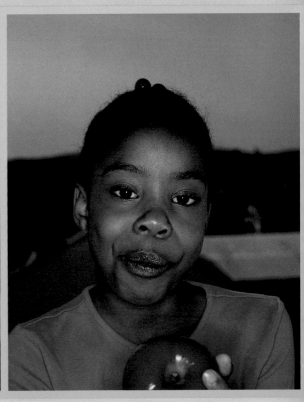

I am
warm apple
pie.

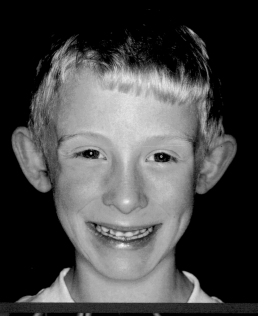

I am

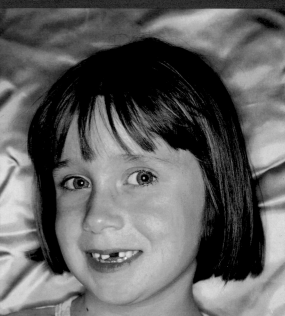

Catholic,
Protestant,
Muslim, Jewish.

Christian,
Mormon,
Quaker, Amish.

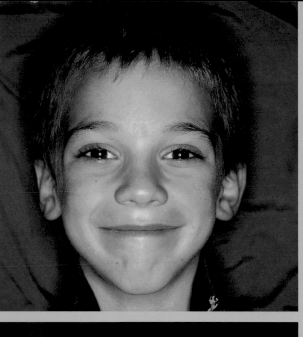

I
am

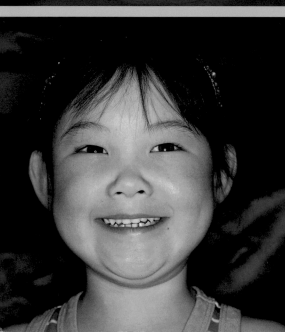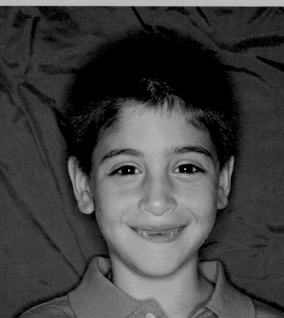

Asian, Italian,
Indian, Irish.

Greek, Latino,
African, Polish.

I am
a new branch
sprouting

in my majestic family tree.

and
America
is me.